Sara grew up not knowing how to talk about her feelings, so she started writing as a means of escape, or more specifically to say what she couldn't say out loud. She started her writing journey writing paragraphs and later got into free-verse poetry, which she fell in love with. The poetry found in this book is her way of seeing the world. Some poems talk about her experiences as a young adult and others talk about her thoughts on certain areas of life. This book is her way of expressing herself in a way she never thought she could.

To myself. To my parents for always supporting me. To my siblings for making me laugh till I'm in tears. To my closest friends for being my partners in crime, and finally, to all the people who made me feel those emotions and inspired me to write them down.

Sara Alblooshi

PROFUNDITY

AUSTIN MACAULEY PUBLISHERS™

LONDON • CAMBRIDGE • NEW YORK • SHARJAH

ISBN – 9789948797456 – (Paperback)
ISBN – 9789948797463 – (E-Book)

Application Number: MC-10-01-4652912
Age Classification: E

First Published 2023
AUSTIN MACAULEY PUBLISHERS FZE
Sharjah Publishing City
P.O Box [519201]
Sharjah, UAE
www.austinmacauley.ae
+971 655 95 202

To my parents, brothers, and sister, thank you for supporting me with your love and presence in my life.

To Miss Lynette, my English teacher for 10 years, thank you for educating me the right way regardless of all the hardships you went through. Thank you for your love and support.

To my friends, thank you for never letting me give up writing and for always supporting my dreams.

To myself, thank you for staying strong even in your worst moments. Look at you now!

Finally, I would like to express my love and appreciation to anyone who acknowledges the feelings I poured into these poems.

Thank you!

Broken Mind

all i see is you.
get out!
stop racing through a broken mind
you can't rectify it.
are you blind
not to see what you're doing
or are you just unkind?
drugs are supposed to ease your mind,
makes you stop thinking
or so i was told
but all it perpetrates to me
is clear everything out of my mind
and leaves you the pivot of my reckless mind
and we all know how that goes down.
illusions of you make me lose my mind
thinking you actually cared is a curse
but i can't break free
i love you, damn it
but you're not worth the agony
nor the effort
stop racing through my broken mind
you'll lose nothing
but i'll lose my sanity
trying to hold on to you.

I Saw the Pain

i saw the pain in your eyes
and all i could do
was be in pain
i thought i could heal you
but the truth is you healed me
the pain in your eyes helped me
become stronger
and now it's my turn to heal you.
i saw the pain in your eyes
but I can't heal you if you don't allow me.

Chase Love*?*

i'd never chase love
i'd let it come to me
said a girl
but she never knew
what love actually was
she thought love can be controlled and measured.
she thought she knew
but was far from knowing
she thought she felt
but was far from feeling
she was a young teen who mistook crushing for loving.
she ran around saying
"how could you do that just for love?"
"why are you chasing him?"
"he's not worth it"
but then karma did what it had to
and made her fall in love
to make her understand the people she mocked
what they felt and how they felt it
so she learns not to judge without feeling,
without experiencing
the people she said she'll never be like
are just like her now.

Stars

they say
someone will come
and light up the darkness
in your sky with their stars
i replied
why wait for someone
when i can light up
my own sky with my own stars.

Math

13

maybe i'm right
maybe i'm wrong
you leave me in such a confusion
i don't understand
but i do
just like Math.

Instability

i'm about to fall
i'm with no aid
i can't concentrate
i feel so disconnected
they're advocating me
to be someone i'm not
but oh wait
that's their nature
to eradicate all aspiration
to produce a world stacked
with identical souls and minds
why are we here
to wreck ourselves
to wound others
maybe both
but that's only what they anticipate
how about the factual cause of us being here
instead of thinking of that
we strive to alter people to our likings
we were never meant to be the same
yet we kill to be parallel
because that in their eyes is equality
what a never-ending diversion
i'm about to fall

but there's a never-ending pit
i can't run away and i can't remain.

I know people believe in heroes

but all i wanna believe in is
you.

Flames

heat is rising
heartbeat racing
we are about to burn this city
with the flames of our souls
burning what's right and wrong
what's logical and realistic
ignoring the truth
and all i'm looking for
is your flame
for it's the only thing
that can burn me along.

I Always Wonder

i don't know what to believe
your words or your actions
i can't blame you
because i do the same
say something and then do something else
but that's because i don't know
if you care as much as i do
and I always wonder if you're the same.

Speak Up Sky

the night sky is gazing upon me
rivers flowing from my eyes
and the moon is watching
how much pain i've endured
i know i'm supposed to speak up
and let them know
but damn
i think explaining is the hardest
task of them all
cause how will they believe
when they haven't seen.
the night sky is gazing upon me
the sky is the only one who knows it all
the silent breaking
the heart aching
the chest narrowing
too bad it can't speak
it has all the secrets of the universe
yet people still think it's just beautiful.
it's another dimension
full of enigmas and hidden truths
speak up sky

we're all exhausted
no one believes us but you

Why do we always try to solve the problems that don't even
exist yet?

We keep on trying to find solutions to the problems of the
future
Maybe it's just our getaway
for the problems happening now.

No Sense at All

when everything makes total sense
why are we still lost?
when everything is falling into place
what's that empty space in the middle?
why is it that when we think we are complete
we realize we will never fully be?

Means of Escape

are we trying to find a way
are we listening to our hearts
or are we just trying to escape logic?
are we really who we say we are
are we really here to love
or are we here to forget?

Unexplainable Talks

silent talks
talking eyes
all i have to do
is look deep
and you'll be everything
i can't explain.

Goodbye

it was time
time to say goodbye
but i couldn't look
i was too scared
to look into your eyes
and find the calmness i was lost in
knowing that they were
never to be seen again.

Reborn

can i cry
and empty my soul
but what if it's already empty
will i turn into nothing
or will i feel again
will you touch my emptiness
and turn it into something
that can heal by time
or will you add salt to the wound?
you are just like the others
but different than all
you were my weakness all along
but it's now that i realized
how deep you can hurt.
can i cry
and empty my soul
will i turn into dust
or will i be reborn?

Surreal Experience

can we run away
to another dimension
nah that's a cliche
let's run to our minds
where yours is full of me
and mine is full of yours
it's another facet
of surreal experience
where we only exist
and the fundaments of it
are our desires
they say we only live once
but i say we can live forever
in each other's minds.

What Is a Mess?

you want to know what's a mess
when reality mixes up with your thoughts
when you don't know what's real
and what's not
when you are stuck in the middle
and you need to believe a side
but both look logical
you see thoughts as reality
and reality as thoughts
you look around
nothing makes sense
but at the same time
it's the perfect amount of sense
that's a mess
when your sanity is threatened
and all you can do is feel lost
that's a mess
and when you finally reach peace
that's when you lose it all

Why is hope so important if it doesn't lead me to
YOU?

What If

29

i know we were not meant to be
but what if were
i know it's too late
but what if it's not
i know you thought you're done
but what if i'm not
a series of i knows
and a series of what ifs
we no longer know what to believe in
and that's because
what if it's wrong.

Path Before You

i thought i was lost
but it's when i met you
that i knew
i was never even close
you made me lose my path
you were the distraction
i tried being lost with you
but you pushed me away
and so I was lost all alone
i'm back on my path
my path before you
cause baby:
nunca es tarde para aprender. *

*Spanish Proverb: It's never too late to learn

how is it so hard to forget
              but so easy to remember?

And I Fell

i fell on the ground
my heart pumping blood
outside my body
i look around and found all the people
roaming around me
watching me
no one dares to give a hand
do i deserve to feel pain
in such a corrupt society?
do i deserve the blames
that are not heard but known?
do i deserve feeling this unloved
in a society that claims to be filled with love?
why is it
that decent people never get what they deserve
or are we just the run-ons
the ones you step on
do i deserve to feel this broken
when all i do is fix people?
do i deserve to feel happy
or is that not on the list of societal standards
are you people humans with feelings
and we're robots with broken wires?

Memories

33

Are they a curse or a blessing?

Time

how long did it take me
to forget all those memories?
to finally be me again
i don't know anymore
i've lost count of the times i've returned
hoping something changed.
time heals everything they say
truth is
we heal ourselves
we use time to our advantage
but somehow all the credit goes to "time"
i can't help but remember the countless times
i said there's no way i can live without your presence
and months passed
what i said was accurate
but only because I believed so
the moment i believed the opposite
i was living my best life without you
time
it can be used for you
or against you
or by you.

Pawn

it's funny how i couldn't imagine
a life without you
damn I had no clue
about the path I was gonna go through

I thought I wouldn't be able to breathe
but look at me now
breathing as if I always knew how
maybe even better

thought you taught me happiness
when all you did
is allow me to forbid
happiness if it ain't with you

I'm happier than ever now
without you
like I should've grew
because happiness is me

damn everyone who taught me
that happiness is in things or in a person
they only allowed me to worsen
and think I was the reason
to all the pains I've seen

not you, not my own bloodline
can make me believe
that I can't achieve
the happiness i want and need

kill me once
shame on you
kill me twice, it's overdue
you only want happiness for you

sharing is caring they say
guess they couldn't apply
but they didn't even try
cause that's how deranged they are

you're my blood
but happiness is mine
I don't care if you die
you're only a pawn
and i care about the prize

well guess what
your pawn found the prize
and she's beginning to rise
she'll be the happiness
and she'll teach it too

one loss is nothing
compared to the edge
let me make this pledge
I'll keep fighting
till I see happiness all around me.

Hodri Meydan

all the voices
saying it's all over
but we both know it's not
the end is usually
not the end
and not even a beginning
it's a chance
a chance to save your soul.
it's funny that it never runs out
which is why we use it
to save people
instead of ourselves.

all the voices
saying you got no one
but we both know you don't need 'em
people are there
to give and take
some take more than they give
and some give more than they take
they both end up crying
one out of misery from "loneliness"
and the other out of exhaust
what a strange world
you're always alone

yet you fool yourself
by saying "they're there for me"
the world is playing us all
with its beliefs, standards, and conceptions
but in Turkish there's a phrase that goes
"hodri meydan" which means I dare you
so life
here I am
I think you've broken me enough
with your lies, people, and shit
but
hodri meydan.

Don't You Know*?*

don't you know how much it hurts
that you are no longer here
and what's worse
is that you never cared
i was always right
but never about you.
it hurts to know
i am the best at fixing people
but so bad at fixing me
that I easily help with other's feelings
but so hardly with me
i gave up trying
but you taught me trying in another way.
now that you're gone
I don't see the point of
believing it's worth it
cause you ended up making me
give up
and not only in trying
but in pure love
what's the point of loving
when no one gives it back?

what's the point of hoping
when at the end it's a shock?

what's the point of trying to feel
when at the end you're full of pain
way more than what you started with
no point
no meaning
as if the world was made
from pure blankness
and you're supposed to fill it up
but when you do
they call it a mess.

The Only Edge

on the edge,
the edge of losing me again.
for people,
again.
how do I constantly find myself here,
as if there's no other diversion?
this test never ends.
the temptation
of losing it,
losing everything again,
is way more vast
than my own will to live.
but isn't that the point,
isn't that what they want?
to end my life
by making me resent existence.
easy concept,
make me a zombie
and expect me to accept it.
guess there's no way to end this test,
other than destroying it
by breathing even more
along while loving it.
looking them in the eye
and saying

"I've never been more alive."

It Is What It Is

in a time of uncertainty,
it is ironic to be so certain
about how I want to live my life,
who to love
and where to go.

in a time of uncertainty,
I've never felt more alive.
I've never been in this many
adventures, until now.

in a time of uncertainty,
everyone left
when they were expected to stay
but the real ones came out.

in a time of uncertainty,
I remembered who I am
my pains, traumas, childhood
and I came out stronger than ever.

in a time of uncertainty,
I realized I breathed air with cowards
and said it is what it is
but decided that it isn't what it is

and did whatever made me vibrant.

in a time of uncertainty,
where I was supposed to lose hope.
the unexplainable certainty
of feeling enthusiastic in such time
made me love the fickleness of life.

The List

feelings increase
I don't know if it's me
or is it normal to never belong
as if I'm an outcast of this world

it's me
then it's not
maybe it's just that I don't agree
with the norms that they think they show love

why am I cursed with such pain
as if no one understands
and as I drain out of humanity
they ignore me as if I'm insane

is it just now
or did I always flinch
whenever someone showed me some care.
did I always ask about the behind the scenes
when someone tries to show me they want to
show love?

what should I do
when I am scared to talk it out
because I know their reaction would be

"I understand" but they most certainly do not.
they explain what I say in what they think
I went through, not the way I did

I believe in humanity still
but the day I lose hope
and go back to being a soulless body,
know that
I'm tired of always being last
or not included in the list.

Riddle

feeling stuck
feeling misunderstood
all the creatures align
but we still have no luck

how are we supposed to be known
when all around us think we're lost
"oh we know what you feel"
if you did we wouldn't be alone

few people look around and say what if
but the people surrounding us
think that they're the all-knowing
please come take me I need a lift

I zone out in the middle of gatherings
and they ask, "are you with us?"
I look around and can't help but see
the gradual scattering

how can it be that in a room
full of laughter, people with such impure hearts
wait so eagerly
to see others in a tomb

why is it that when we point out the truth
in a space where it should be filled with it
because of the amount of "grown-ups"
we're called the uneducated youth

if adults are supposed to be our idols
the ones who are mature
and live life so flawlessly as said
why are we the rivals

in a world of such toxicity
where ideas are eliminated
just 'cause it doesn't fit the adults' standards
why do they blame us for our simplicity

"your generation thinks everything is simple"
have you thought why
maybe our minds are open to solutions
rather than problems that only riddle

we live in a world where it's a sin to think
because what if the adults disagree
our lives are under constant consent
of people who are scared to blink

respect is essential
but a riddle is only solved
when you understand it
so let us live how we understand
and avoid the unwanted tension

the difference of our generation
should not threaten you
we live for ourselves with advice
that we choose to take or not
because in the end it's our formation.

Consistency

consistency
something far away than what we have learned
they made us absorb the fact that inconsistency is how we
deserve to be treated but we're sick of not knowing the things
we're supposed to know
i hear the inner children's cries for help
knowing pain never leaves
and inconsistency is the base of it
being lost?
feeling unwanted?
having low self-esteem?
all because of inconsistency.
we are in a world where having
two or more faces is encouraged
and being true is being abrupt.
inconsistency makes us fall in a hole
and get back to fall in another
yet somehow it's how life is lived "maturely"
it's how our adults explain life.
how can they not realize the toxicity
it's why our adults scream
"you take life so easily, it's not that easy"
because we want consistency in our lives
we want solutions for our inner children
rather than inconsistency that kills them.

No Good in This World

it's such a torment
when you scream of pain
yet no one seems to listen
and if they do
they close their ears

it's such an agony
that the people who you helped with a full heart
laugh at the scene of your soul crying
like it's a joke

it's such a disappointment
when the people you thought
won't be fooled by your happy mask
were the ones ignoring your pain,
in fact they only make it worse

no wonder people say
there's no good in this world
the only good you find is when it benefits them
i need attention, yeah let's be on good terms with her
i need answers, yeah let's stay friends with her
life is getting harder by the second
no, sorry
people are getting harder to deal with by the second

and the problem is you can't cut off everyone
without feeling like you're gonna go insane.

Coffee Break

in a world filled with coffee pictures,
fake smiles,
and an addiction to showing off,
i choose happiness
i choose life
i choose pictures that are never posted
love that's never showed off
i choose peace of mind
and an addiction to being exclusive
what life are we choosing to live in?
a life where insincerity is praised
and sincerity is criticized?
"you don't know how to live."
no, I just like to live on my own terms happily
and not on others' terms
with an imitation of happily ever after.
so let's take a coffee break,
don't forget to show off where you got it from,
while I sip and mesmerize that taste of it.

Lost in a world filled with my own FANTASIES.

THE END

9 789948 797456